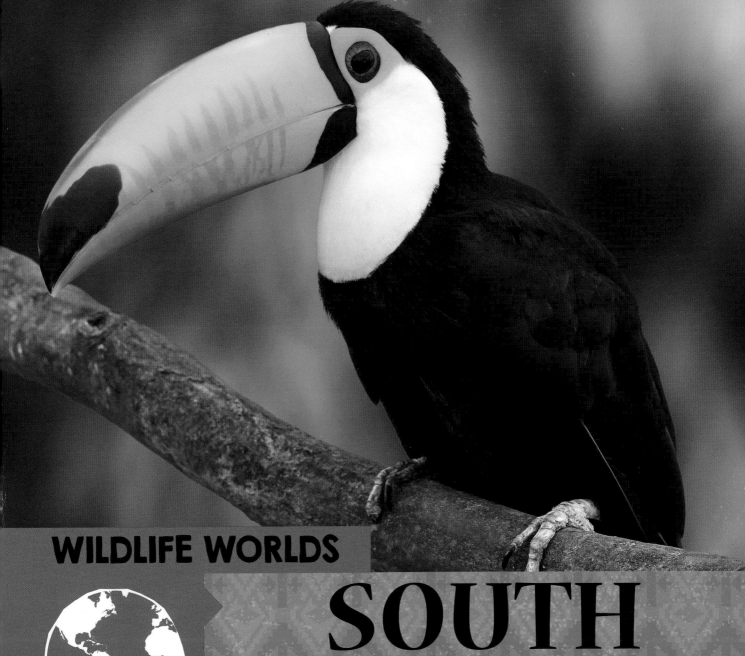

WILDLIFE WORLDS

SOUTH AMERICA

TIM HARRIS

CRABTREE
PUBLISHING COMPANY
WWW.CRABTREEBOOKS.COM

CRABTREE
PUBLISHING COMPANY
WWW.CRABTREEBOOKS.COM

Published in Canada
Crabtree Publishing
616 Welland Avenue
St. Catharines, ON
L2M 5V6

Published in the United States
Crabtree Publishing
PMB 59051
350 Fifth Ave, 59th Floor
New York, NY 10118

Published in 2020 by Crabtree Publishing Company

First published in Great Britain in 2019 by The Watts Publishing Group
Copyright © The Watts Publishing Group 2019

Printed in the U.S.A./122019/CG20191101

With thanks to the Nature Picture Library

Author: Tim Harris

Editorial director: Kathy Middleton

Editors: Amy Pimperton, Robin Johnson

Series Designer: Nic Davies
smartdesignstudio.co.uk

Photo researchers: Rachelle Morris (Nature Picture Library), Laura Sutherland (Nature Picture Library), Diana Morris

Proofreader: Wendy Scavuzzo

Prepress: Tammy McGarr

Print and production coordinator: Katherine Berti

Every attempt has been made to clear copyright. Should there be any inadvertent omission, please apply to the publisher for rectification.

Photo credits:
Alamy: Dani Carlo/Prisma/Dukas Presseagentur GmbH 21bl.
Dreamstime: Agami Photo Agency 15b; Anky10 25tl; Maria Luisa Lopez Estivill 19c; David Havel 8br, 31t; Izanbar 25tc; Laura Kanda 10; Jesse Kraft 14bl; Mikelane45 22bl; Ondrej Prosicky 23bl; Jeremy Richards 21tr; Gabriel Rojo 26bl; Scanrail 1, 23br; Sietebravo 3t, 11c; Taani65 22br.
FLPA Images: Malcolm Schuyl 19br.
Nature PL: Oriol Alamany 28; Theo Allofs 22–23; Juan Manuel Borrero 27t Mark Bowler 25bt; Lucas Bustamante 19tr; Bernard Castelein 17c; Murray Cooper/Minden 12; Christophe Courteau 7c; Jack Dykinga 21c; Nick Hawkins front cover t; Daniel Heuclin 8bl; Chien Lee/Minden 25bl; Luiz Claudio Marigo 16; David Noton 2b, 18–19c, 20; Pete Oxford 8–9c, 17bc; Michael Pitts 29bl; Michel Roggo back cover tcl, 24; Gabriel Rojo 15tr, 26c, 27bl; Andy Rouse 11t; Cyril Ruoso 15tl; Kevin Schafer 7tr; Roland Seitre 27br; Visuals Unlimited 13bl; David Welling 9tr; Staffan Widstrand 23tr; Bert Willaert 17br.
Shutterstock: abriendomundo 21br,31b; Audrey Snider-Bell 9br; tamara bizjak 11bl; Ger Bosma Photos 13tr, 30b; buteo back cover tl, 7tl; Patrick K Campbell 6b; Ecuadorpostales 14c; Dirk Ercken front cover b, 4b; Andrey Golinkevich 6–7; guentermanaus 13tl; Lukasz Kurbiel 2t, 17t, 30c; Lucas Leuzinger back cover tcr, 4c, 30t; Lulilel front cover c; Don Mammoser 3cr, 11br; MarcusVDT 3br, 25tr; Veronika Maskova 5c; Carlos Mauer 29tr; Vadim Petrakov 5t; Anton Petrus 3bg, 4–5bg, 29t, 30bg; Eduardo Rivero 29br; Miroslaw Skorka 19tl; Super Prin back cover tr, 5b, 13br; Wollertz 17bl.

Library and Archives Canada Cataloguing in Publication

Title: South America / Tim Harris.
Names: Harris, Tim (Ornithologist), author.
Description: Series statement: Wildlife worlds |
  Previously published: London: Franklin Watts, 2019. | Includes index.
Identifiers: Canadiana (print) 20190200693 |
  Canadiana (ebook) 20190200707 |
  ISBN 9780778776826 (hardcover) |
  ISBN 9780778777045 (softcover) |
  ISBN 9781427125361 (HTML)
Subjects: LCSH: Animals—South America—Juvenile literature. |
  LCSH: Habitat (Ecology)—South America—Juvenile literature. |
  LCSH: Natural history—South America—Juvenile literature. |
  LCSH: South America—Juvenile literature.
Classification: LCC QL235 .H37 2020 | DDC j591.98—dc23

Library of Congress Cataloging-in-Publication Data

Names: Harris, Tim (Ornithologist), author.
Title: Wildlife worlds South America / Tim Harris.
Description: New York : Crabtree Publishing Company, 2020. |
  Series: Wildlife worlds | Includes index.
Identifiers: LCCN 2019043858 (print) | LCCN 2019043859 (ebook) |
  ISBN 9780778776826 (hardcover) |
  ISBN 9780778777045 (paperback) |
  ISBN 9781427125361 (ebook)
Subjects: LCSH: Animals--South America--Juvenile literature. | Habitat
  (Ecology)--South America--Juvenile literature. | Rain forest animals-
  -Amazon River Region--Juvenile literature. | Plants--South America--
  Juvenile literature. | South America--Juvenile literature.
Classification: LCC QL235 .H39 2020 (print) | LCC QL235 (ebook) |
  DDC 591.98--dc23
LC record available at https://lccn.loc.gov/2019043858
LC ebook record available at https://lccn.loc.gov/2019043859

Contents

South American Continent

South America is almost completely surrounded by oceans. Its only link to land is the Isthmus of Panama, which connects it to Central America. South America's incredible geography boasts the longest mountain range and the biggest river by water volume, which is surrounded by the world's largest rain forest.

South America is a continent of extremes. Some of the rainiest places on Earth are found near the Pacific coast of Colombia, while it never rains in parts of the Atacama Desert. The continent's varied landforms and climates, combined with the fact that large areas have not been disturbed much by humans, mean that South America's nature is very diverse. There are more kinds of birds and amphibians there than in any other continent, though many are **endangered**.

More than 2.5 million species of plants and animals are believed to live in the Amazon rain forest alone. Scientists think this figure could be even higher.

JAGUAR

GOLDEN DART FROG

4

Angel Falls has the highest uninterrupted drop of any waterfall on Earth.

ANGEL FALLS

Llanos

Isthmus of Panama

Galapagos Islands

Andes Mountains

Lake Titicaca

Atacama Desert

South Pacific Ocean

Torres del Paine

North Atlantic Ocean

Orinoco River

Tepuis

Guiana Highlands

Equator

Amazon River

Amazon Rain Forest and Amazon River Basin

Altiplano

The Pantanal is the world's largest freshwater wetland.

Iguazú Falls

Paraguay River

Iguazú River

Pampas

Pampas

South Atlantic Ocean

SCARLET MACAW

5

Llanos

The Llanos is a vast area of **tropical** grassland broken up by patches of forest. It stretches from the Colombian **foothills** of the Andes Mountains to the **delta** of the Orinoco River in Venezuela.

The Llanos is dry for much of the year. But when heavy rains start in April, the rivers that flow into the Orinoco burst their banks. Then the area becomes a series of huge, shallow lakes. These lakes are perfect feeding areas for birds and reptiles, including the world's most powerful snake—the green anaconda.

Up to 300,000 herons, storks, waterfowl, and shorebirds feed on the Llanos wetland.

Green anacondas kill their **prey** by squeezing them to death. They can kill animals as large as deer and capybaras.

The capybara is the world's largest rodent. It spends most of its life in water.

Rare pink river dolphins can be found in the waters of the Llanos.

A giant anteater has an incredibly long, sticky tongue. It uses its tongue to pull up to 30,000 ants from their nests each day.

Tepuis

A series of large, flat-topped mountains called tepuis are found in parts of Venezuela and nearby countries. The word *tepui* means "house of the gods" in the language of the local Pemon people.

The tepuis are made of tough, ancient **sandstone** and tower high above the surrounding rain forest. The plant and animal life on the mountaintops is very different from that in the forest below. Some plants growing on the **summits** exist nowhere else on Earth. There are no large animals at the top of the tepuis, but plenty of birds, frogs, and mice live there.

Pale-throated sloths live on the lower slopes of the mountains. They sleep for up to 20 hours each day, hanging from branches. When the sloths move, they move very slowly.

A beautifully marked but highly **venomous** snake called the fer-de-lance lives in the forests below the tepuis.

Angel Falls is the world's highest waterfall. Water from the Churún River plunges 3,212 feet (979 m) from the top of the Auyán-tepui in Venezuela to form the waterfall.

Goliath birdeaters are the largest spiders in the world. They eat frogs, small mammals, and lizards, but, despite their name, they only rarely kill birds.

Galapagos Islands

The Galapagos Islands lie on both sides of the equator in the Pacific Ocean and are part of Ecuador. These islands were created by millions of years of volcanic **eruptions** and are made up of **lava**. Almost all the reptiles, most of the land birds, and one-third of the plants on the islands, are found nowhere else on Earth.

Reptiles on the islands include giant Galapagos tortoises, which can live to be more than 100 years old. Many seabirds raise their young on the islands, including Galapagos penguins. These birds are the only members of their family found north of the equator.

Galapagos penguins hunt small fish in the cold, nutrient-rich Cromwell **Current** during the day and return to the islands at night.

Sally Lightfoot crabs are brightly colored **scavengers** that live on the shore of the Galapagos Islands.

A male blue-footed booby dances, showing off his feet to impress a female. Brighter blue feet are more attractive to females.

Marine iguanas graze on **algae** that grows on underwater rocks. They then swim ashore to warm their bodies in the sunshine.

11

Amazon Rain Forest

The Amazon is the world's largest tropical rain forest. It covers an area of 2.3 million square miles (6 million square km) and stretches across eight South American countries. This massive forest contains 390 billion trees in 16,000 different species.

With 2.5 million plant and animal species, the Amazon rain forest has the greatest variety of living things on Earth. Noisy rainbow-colored macaws and other parrots fly through the forest canopy. Up there, monkeys and sloths stay hidden most of the time to avoid hungry harpy eagles. Down below, crocodiles and piranhas search for prey in rivers, while jaguars and wild cats called ocelots prowl the forest floor.

The Amazon River drains the rain forest, carrying its excess water to the Atlantic Ocean. This river carries more water than the next seven biggest rivers put together.

The **transparent** wings of glasswing butterflies help hide them from birds and other **predators** in the rain forest.

Fish called piranhas have sharp teeth and strong jaws to eat unlucky animals that get too close!

Brightly colored poison dart frogs live in plants called bromeliads that grow on tall rainforest trees.

Scarlet macaws are colorful, noisy birds that eat seeds, nuts, and fruit growing on forest trees.

Andes Mountains

The Andes are the longest mountain range in the world. They stretch about 4,500 miles (7,240 km) from the southern tip of Argentina to the northern part of Colombia.

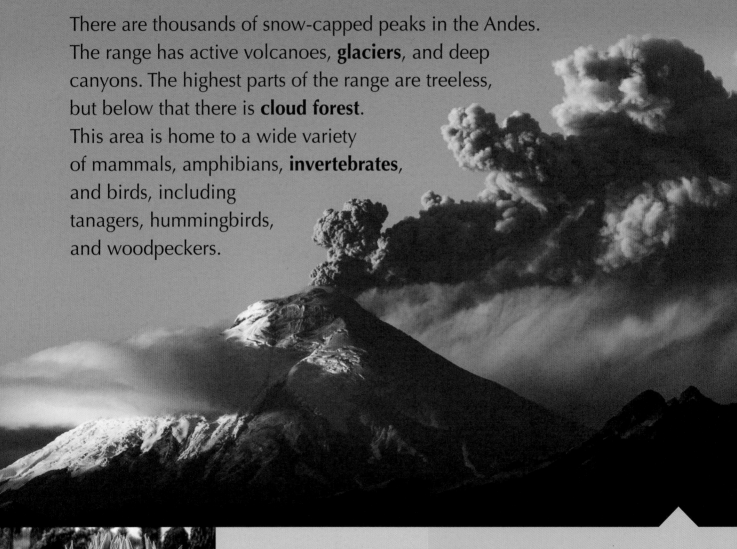

There are thousands of snow-capped peaks in the Andes. The range has active volcanoes, **glaciers**, and deep canyons. The highest parts of the range are treeless, but below that there is **cloud forest**. This area is home to a wide variety of mammals, amphibians, **invertebrates**, and birds, including tanagers, hummingbirds, and woodpeckers.

Espeletias are found high in the Andes. These plants have thick trunks that take in water from nearby clouds that drift by.

Famous peaks in the Andes include Cotopaxi (above) and Aconcagua. Cotopaxi is one of the world's highest active volcanoes. Aconcagua rises higher than any other mountain outside of Asia.

Shy vicuñas live in herds on high mountain slopes. People sometimes use them for their very fine wool.

The Andean cock-of-the-rock is a cloud forest bird. Males gather in groups and display their brilliant feathers, bowing and flapping to attract the attention of females.

Andean condors are the largest flying land birds in the world. They often fly more than 124 miles (200 km) a day in search of dead animals to eat, rarely flapping their wings.

Lake Titicaca

Lake Titicaca is an amazing body of fresh water. It is the largest lake in South America. At 12,500 feet (3,810 m) above sea level, it is also the highest large lake in the world.

Lake Titicaca is located high in the Andes Mountains on the border between Bolivia and Peru. Many rivers drain into the lake but only one, the Desaguadero River, flows out. **Reedbeds** and other **aquatic** plants grow around the lake, providing shelter for fish and frogs to breed and for birds to build their nests. Almost all of Titicaca's fish species live nowhere else in the world.

Isla del Sol, or Island of the Sun, is the largest of the 41 islands in the lake. Most people who live there are farmers and fishers. The island's many ruins date back hundreds of years to the **Inca** civilization.

Culpeos, or Andean foxes, hunt rabbits and other small animals.

The cantuta has bright-pink, trumpet-shaped flowers. It is the national flower of Peru.

Local people build boats and even houses from the totora reeds that grow around the lake.

Titicaca water frogs spend most of their lives at the bottom of the lake. Like all frogs, their skin can take in **oxygen** from the water.

17

Altiplano

The Altiplano, or "high plain," is a vast windswept **plateau** of grassland, sparkling white **salt flats**, and lakes high above sea level. Oxygen levels in the air are only half those at sea level.

The Altiplano lies between two massive ranges of the Andes in Bolivia and Chile. Many of the surrounding mountains are active volcanoes. Although warm during the day, temperatures often plunge below freezing at night. It rarely rains. Despite these difficult conditions, many animals live there, including members of the camel family called llamas, vicuñas, and alpacas. The lakes attract large flocks of flamingos and ducks.

A lake called Laguna Miscanti lies in a valley surrounded by bunch grass below the **extinct** volcano of Cerro Miscanti. The lake is more than 13,123 feet (4,000 m) above sea level, which is higher than Lake Titicaca.

One of the rarest birds in the world, the Andean flamingo, breeds at just a few shallow lakes, including Laguna Colorada.

Spectacled bears usually live alone. They eat mostly plants, but they also kill and eat rabbits and other small animals.

CERRO MISCANTI

The Andean hillstar hummingbird feeds on the **nectar** of flowering plants, including prickly cacti.

Like all cacti, the candelabra cactus thrives in very dry places. It grows up to 20 feet (6 m) tall. This plant has a spiny trunk and tube-shaped white flowers.

Atacama Desert

Sandwiched between the Andes Mountains and the Pacific Ocean in northern Chile is the Atacama Desert, the driest desert on Earth. On average, only 0.6 inches (1.5 cm) of rain falls there each year. In some parts of the desert, no rain has fallen for many years.

Despite its very dry climate, more than 500 different kinds of plants have been found growing in the Atacama Desert. Cacti and **succulents** store what little water is available to help them survive. **Hardy** animals such as scorpions, beetles, and lizards can also survive in this desert. Humboldt penguins live along the Pacific shore, and flamingos breed at the salty lakes that form in a salt flat in the desert.

The *Valle de la Luna*, or Valley of the Moon, got its name because it looks like the surface of the moon.

With its big ears and strong hind legs, a viscacha looks like a rabbit with a long tail.

Burrowing owls rest in holes in the ground. They often move into holes left by viscachas.

The Fabian's lizard is found only in the Salar de Atacama, a huge salt flat in the desert.

When rain falls, plants sprout and bloom as if by magic in a vivid show of color called the desierto florido, or "desert bloom."

Pantanal

Covering an area more than 69,500 square miles (180,000 square km) in size, the Pantanal is the world's largest freshwater wetland. It lies on the **floodplain** of the Paraguay River, which drains much of southern Brazil.

When heavy rains fall between November and March, vast areas of grassland and forest are flooded. Water levels go down during the dry season, but many swamps and **marshes** remain. These are home to millions of waterbirds and large reptiles called caimans, as well as big cats, crab-eating foxes, and marsh deer.

Pig-like tapirs are excellent at swimming and diving.

The sunbittern spreads its wings and shows spots that look like eyes to surprise predators.

Water levels rise by about 16 feet (5 m) in the wet season. Some areas are completely flooded with water, while large lakes appear in other areas.

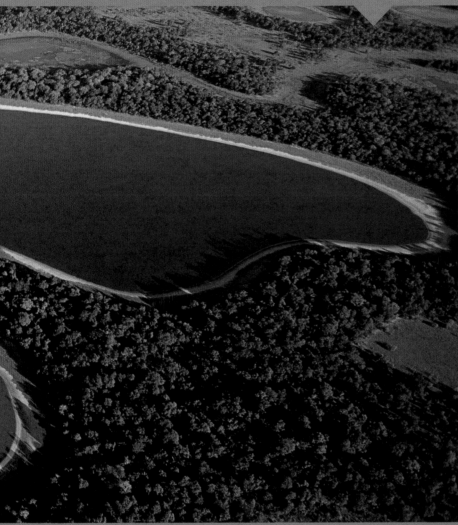

Jaguars are the biggest wild cats in South America. They can kill any other animals living in the Pantanal, except the largest caimans.

As many as 10 million yacare caimans live in the Pantanal. This is the largest population of **crocodilians** anywhere in the world.

A toucan's large beak is designed to lose body heat, which helps keep the bird cool.

Iguazú Falls

On the border between Argentina and Brazil, the mighty Iguazú River flows over a layer of very hard rock. When the water reaches the edge, it crashes 269 feet (82 m) down as the Iguazú Falls.

The Iguazú Falls are one of the biggest waterfall systems in the world. On average, 3.5 million cubic feet (100 million l) of water flows over them every minute. That is enough water to fill 40 Olympic swimming pools! The spray soaks the area around the falls, nourishing the forest. In turn, the trees provide homes for frogs, insects, birds, and other animals.

When water levels are high in the Iguazú River, it may plunge over as many as 300 separate falls, producing clouds of spray as it roars through a **chasm** called the Devil's Throat.

Many kinds of butterflies live near the falls, including a species called Cramer's eighty-eight. They are named for the markings on the undersides of their wings.

The harpy eagle is a powerful bird. It can grab a monkey from the forest canopy and fly away with it.

Black capuchin monkeys are one of the smartest monkey species in South America.

Ring-tailed coatis are members of the raccoon family. They are equally at home on the ground or climbing around in trees.

A bullet ant's sting is the most painful of any insect.

Pampas

Stretching from the foothills of the Andes Mountains to the Atlantic coast in Argentina is a vast plain of grassland called the Pampas. The word *pampa* means "flat surface" in Spanish.

Although many of the original rough grasses have been replaced by those more suited to the cattle raised there, the Pampas is still important for many wild mammals, birds, and reptiles. Large wildfires burn the grass regularly, but it grows back quickly.

Pampas foxes live in dens in hollow trees or in holes dug by other animals.

Darwin's rhea cannot fly, but it can run up to 37 miles per hour (60 kph) to escape a predator. Male birds **incubate** the eggs and guard the chicks for about six weeks after they hatch.

Pampas grass is **native** to the region. It can grow up to 10 feet (3 m) high and has distinctive white feathery blooms.

Geoffroy's cats are about the size of house cats, but they are wild animals that hunt alone at night.

Torres del Paine

Near the Pacific coast in the far south of Chile is one of the most spectacular landscapes on Earth. The Torres del Paine are jagged peaks of rock that tower over the surrounding countryside.

The Torres del Paine National Park is named for these impressive peaks. The Spanish word *torres* means "towers."

The national park where the Torres del Paine are found also contains glaciers, lakes, valleys, and many other snow-covered mountains whose summits are often hidden in clouds. Cougars are the top predators in the park, and guanacos and endangered deer called huemuls also live there.

The Cuernos del Paine rise more than 6,500 feet (2,000 m) above Lake Nordenskjöld. *Cuernos* means "horns" in Spanish.

Magellanic woodpeckers have black and bright-red feathers. These large birds eat invertebrates that live in trees.

Commerson's dolphins are small and very active marine mammals. They often leap from the water and spin in the air. Sometimes, they even swim upside down!

Guanacos are fast runners and strong swimmers.

Glossary

algae Very small plant-like life-forms

aquatic Living in water

canopy The highest tree branches in a forest

chasm A deep, steep-sided hole or opening in the ground

cloud forest A forest that is covered with low-lying clouds for much of the time

crocodilians A group of large reptiles that includes alligators and crocodiles

current Water that is moving in one direction

delta The area where a river drops mud and sand as it enters a lake or ocean

endangered At risk of dying out forever

eruptions Explosive blasts from volcanoes

extinct No longer active

floodplain The flat area on both sides of a river that may flood when water levels in the river are high

foothills Hilly areas at the base of a mountain range

glacier A large body of ice moving slowly down a valley

hardy Able to survive harsh conditions, such as extreme heat or cold

Inca A civilization that lived in western South America from 1438 to 1533

incubate To sit on an egg to keep it warm before it hatches

invertebrate An animal without a backbone

lava Hot, melted rock that erupts from a volcano

marine Of or from the ocean

marsh An area of soft, wet land with many grasses and other plants

native Living or growing naturally in an area

nectar Sugary liquid found in flowers

oxygen A gas in the air that animals must breathe to survive

plateau High, level ground

predators Animals that kill and eat other animals

prey Animals that are killed and eaten by other animals

reedbeds Large areas of tall, thin grasses called reeds

salt flat An area of flat land covered with a layer of salt

sandstone Rock made of grains of sand or quartz that have been pressed together over time

scavenger An animal that feeds on dead animals

succulents Plants with thick, fleshy leaves or stems that store water

summit The very top

transparent See-through

tropical Relating to the tropics, the areas above and below the equator

venomous Producing chemicals that can injure or kill prey

Further Information

Books

Adamson, Thomas K. *Learning about South America.* Lerner Publishing, 2015.

Esquivel, Gloria Susana. *South America.* Scholastic, 2019.

Hudak, Heather C. *Pathways Through South America.* Crabtree Publishing, 2019.

Rockett, Paul. *Mapping South America.* Crabtree Publishing, 2017.

Websites

www.dkfindout.com/us/earth/continents/south-america/
Lots of interesting and fun facts about Brazil.

www.ducksters.com/geography/southamerica.php
This website has profiles of every country in South America.

www.gowild.wwf.org.uk/americas
Discover more about your favorite animals in these WWF fact files.

www.nationalgeographic.com/animals/index/
Type in the names of animals and get lots of fascinating facts about mammals, reptiles, amphibians, fish, and birds.

Index